OPEN SKIES

Gillie Robic

First Published in 2022
By Live Canon Poetry Ltd
www.livecanon.co.uk

978-1-909703-94-0

A CIP catalogue record for this book is available from the British Library.

OPEN SKIES

Gillie Robic was born in India, an abiding love and influence, and lives in London. She attended the Sorbonne and UCAD in Paris, and the Central School of Art in London. She is a poet, voice artist, puppeteer, director and designer. Her poems have appeared in magazines and anthologies in the UK and the US. She has two collections published by Live Canon - 'Swimming Through Marble' and 'Lightfalls'.

to the lost...

Contents

his

his head is darkness
his body a furnace
his aim obliteration

The coming of spring

She looks out at her winter-ravaged balcony.
Staying out of the cold
she chooses which plants to prune, leave or cull,
but can't face the freezing air.
She sips hot tea and plans the future.

The arch-antagonist surveys his halted ideology.
Happier with the old cold
he chooses which elements to prune, leave or cull,
dispatches his decisions to the freezing front,
inspects his tea leaves, charts the future.

She no longer has a balcony, her shelter shelled and gone,
she's raw in the cold,
carrying motherhood and mother
through breached and freezing air,
snow for water, no maps.

war offices

i. ministry of food

he likes a bloomer
she artisan sourdough
the displaced want bread

ii. built environment

of course shattered glass
but walls   roofs   every building
on the killing ground

iii. forestry commission

woodland once pristine
become ashes and flinders
strobing in cross-fire

iv. joint air quality unit

the thing with feathers
falls silent   falling   falling
from the open skies

the lure of light

beneath a rooflight watch
the cosmos arc the hours
blue yonder-glow of day
at night the sight of stars
the winking height of planes
electric flicker clouds

a million panes of glass
reflect the city's reach
above the shielding glaze
small silhouettes appear
growing down the air

a flight of missiles
                    falls
                        towards the sky
                light
            shatters

ordnance survey along the permanent way

the air is thick
with jabber
half the world turns
a fossil ear
a marble eye
to the other

fingers dither
over hot-spots
here and there
but stab gleefully
into the heart
here
        and there it is
laid bare
the chosen target
puffing across the familiar barren land
scapegoats to the slaughter

cover

the walls and roofs protect her
let her come into her evening shell
and warm it with little occupations
trivialities of love and boredom
quotidian shelter taken for granted

high wind – only an aerial
hurricane – tiles, gutters, cars
earthquake – even the walls
war – everything

cradling a bundle
she rocks by the roadside
back and forth
past and future
the present flayed
untouchable
no little occupations
nothing trivial
quotidian shelter taken

Winter Picnic

This is not the time for picnics
even when it's milder than usual.
Pink mornings bruise easily,
crimson evenings puddle
into sodden tomorrows.
The sun departs too fast,
it's hard packing up in the dark.

Trek back along the shore
without light or purpose,
just the sound of waves.
Phosphorescence winks
out around your boots,
the universe wheels above.
You forget the cold, the month,
the reason you didn't choose
this unreachable spot to die.

Guano Inc.

Why do other birds lose a sense of preservation
in the unnatural quiet of the emptied city?

Ghosted on office windows, their outlines powdered,
they drop in piles of feathers, stunned and dying.

Some birds seem bewildered, moping about
the shattered streets, looking for handouts.

Fools! We starlings know it's time to be pro-active,
to roost comfortably inside the vacant buildings.

My murmuration settles in penthouse opulence
of the CEO of the Bank of Beatitude.

We're good tenants, we've reserved
the Executive Toilets for our rich deposits.

the turning

see how the sky lowers   threatens
what once sheltered beneath green leaves
torn off and gone into darkness falling
menace exposed in an infinite sky

see how god's creatures shrug into winter
nothing to do now but wait for the fall
of ice and a future where everything surely
turns prayerfully back to the blessing of light

see how some miss the moment of turning
sucked in the undertow of the fall
cancelling hope   concussion of darkness
coffined within the day's brief light

see in the silence entropy falling
rot at the root   fire in the sky

distance

in the beginning
he held her close to feel
her light and grace
her heart's motion
he folded her into his brain
merged their cells
the rhythms of their blood

> in the end
> he must send her away
> from him
> at a safer distance
> from harm

resistance

I am the weakest woman on the island

threaten me with violence
        I will scribble a list of traitors
put your blade to my throat
        I will gabble stories to cover tracks
but threaten my family
        I will tell you the truth

        Of course I can lift babies
        I can lift cars off babies
        break offending arms
        carry stretchers
        I can handle multi-axle trucks
        weaponry

you are murderers
I am the weakest woman on the island

curfew

day breaks across our bodies like a wand
casting spells on our distorted sight
till darkness falls upon us at the end

whatever we hold onto shifts like sand
still running through the hour-glass of night
day breaks across our bodies like a wand

wielding threat or magic in its hand
we climb the walls to gain a little height
till darkness falls upon us at the end

if there's a message daylight tries to send
we try whatever motion's apposite
day breaks across our bodies like a wand

that prods us as a too-familiar friend
and puts our equanimity to flight
till darkness falls upon us at the end

where we can seek oblivion to mend
the optical delusions of the light
day breaks across our bodies like a wand
till darkness falls upon us at the end

Storm Challenger

Look, I am here returned
from the fury of the sky! Alone
I stood on the empty field
watching the big clouds boil
and tear open where fire bolted
towards earth and split
in two, one half spearing ground
in front of me, one behind.
I, untouched, stood firm,
challenging the roaring storm.
Now I crackle, I shine electric,
touch me and you may glow.

bunker

we hardly ever see blue any more
unless we paint the walls
the ones we climb
indigo   cobalt   cerulean   turquoise
all the variations of a heaven we can't see

I did try paint – it ran out
half-way across the ceiling
I stuck on blue fabric
a patchwork of silk   brocade   wool   cotton
until damp unfurled streamers soft from above
with no fresh breeze to move them

only every 24 minutes
when the communal air conditioning
hums on   everything stops
we try to remember   before
it clicks off importantly

Grounded

I plan my imaginary garden to transform my cell,
allocate where everything should go,
then continually dig up the plants, good exercise
to confuse my guards, who are discomfited
by my generous use of night soil
that makes everything lush and green.
At night I contemplate my labour, the shadows
of shrubbery, the luxuriant shape of my cell.

Blindfolded

I am standing in front of a solid wall.
It's dark, or maybe I'm masked or blind,
I don't know where is safe but what is safe?

Behind my eyelids
free-floating blobs of optical blue
are the nearest things I have to light.

Maybe there's a way over the top.
What if it stretches to infinity
(wherever that is)?

Maybe there's a giant escalator
like in *A Matter of Life and Death*,
creeping upward to the great and the good.

I should pull myself together,
I am standing in front of a wall
which may be shielding me from the apocalypse.

Tidally Locked

The phases of the moon are dictated
by branches of the trees that hold it
before it reaches synodic earth.

Above the trees the sky, dilated,
stretches towards the moon to fold it
back into itself, pre-birth.

The swelling sky comes closer, closer,
distorts and threatens space and space
changes from velvet to vulcanised,

distends and presses on the ocean,
where the shifty lunar face
gawps back up from its hidden side.

Tautened stars prick and goad,
till the bloated sky explodes.

Point of Departure

He sits beside me deconstructing himself.
The timbre of his voice changes, his shoulders
lift and lower from minute to uncertain minute.
I realise I have to help, to be a prop for the road.
I offer my hand and help him up with a great tenderness
that washes over me at the sight of this newborn.
I take him to the edge of the water, following its lap,
bathe his head and neck and stroke water into his shirt.
For a while he breathes more calmly but then leaps up,
rushes into the night. I follow. He rips off his shirt,
I pick it up, and all the other clothes he sheds
onto the sand I retrieve in the wake of the naked man.
He addresses a tribunal I cannot see, defends himself
from accusations I cannot hear. I take his hand again,
lead him back to the shoreline, we move northwards.

Around midnight we come to the watering rock.
I find the tin ladle and lower its chain into the hole,
feel the coolness of the depths breathe up at me.
We fill our canteens, drink, settle against the rock.
He sleeps, exhausted, but I do not close my eyes.
I watch every particle, try to interpret the colours.
He explodes with energy as sun splits the hills, starts
moving in the wrong direction. I hand him his clothes,
putting them on does not bring back his old self.
We drink, he eats hard tack, we set off northwards.
It should be easier now in daylight, but we see
too much through rock-watered eyes. Booby traps
are everywhere, there's a high whine in the air.
We have to reach the safe house beyond the strand,
recover a sense of place, a new point of departure.